Keep Clean

A Look at Hygiene

by Katie Bagley

Consultants:
Susan Schultz, RN
Wisconsin Public Health Association

Dave Reimann
Public Health Sanitarian
Minnesota Department of Health

Bridgestone Books
an imprint of Capstone Press
Mankato, Minnesota

Bridgestone Books are published by Capstone Press
151 Good Counsel Drive, P.O. Box 669, Mankato, Minnesota 56002
http://www.capstone-press.com

Library of Congress Cataloging-in-Publication Data
Bagley, Katie.
    Keep clean: a look at hygiene/by Katie S. Bagley.
    p.cm.—(Your health)
    Includes bibliographical references and index.
    ISBN 0-7368-0974-0 (hardcover)
    ISBN 0-7368-4448-1 (paperback)
    1. Hygiene—Juvenile literature. 2. Health—Juvenile literature. [1. Cleanliness.
2. Health.] I. Title. II. Series.
RA777 .B32 2002
613—dc21   00-012538

Summary: An introduction to hygiene, including germs, head lice, wearing clean clothes,
        and the importance of washing the body, hands, and hair.

Editorial Credits
Sarah Lynn Schuette, editor; Karen Risch, product planning editor; Linda Clavel, designer
        and illustrator; Jeff Anderson, photo researcher

Photo Credits
Capstone Press/Gary Sundermeyer, cover
Comstock, Inc., 20
EyeWire Images, 1
Gregg R. Andersen, 4, 8, 10, 12, 16
Jessy Robert Dols Photography, 14
Visuals Unlimited/David M. Phillips, 6; Fred E. Hossler, 18

**Bridgestone Books thanks Mari Schuh, Connie Colwell, and Franklin Elementary School,
Mankato, Minnesota, for providing photo shoot locations.**

1 2 3 4 5 6 07 06 05 04 03 02

Table of Contents

Good Hygiene

Practicing good hygiene means keeping clean. You keep clean by washing your body and wearing clean clothes. Practicing good hygiene helps keep you healthy and looking nice.

hygiene
the actions people take to keep clean

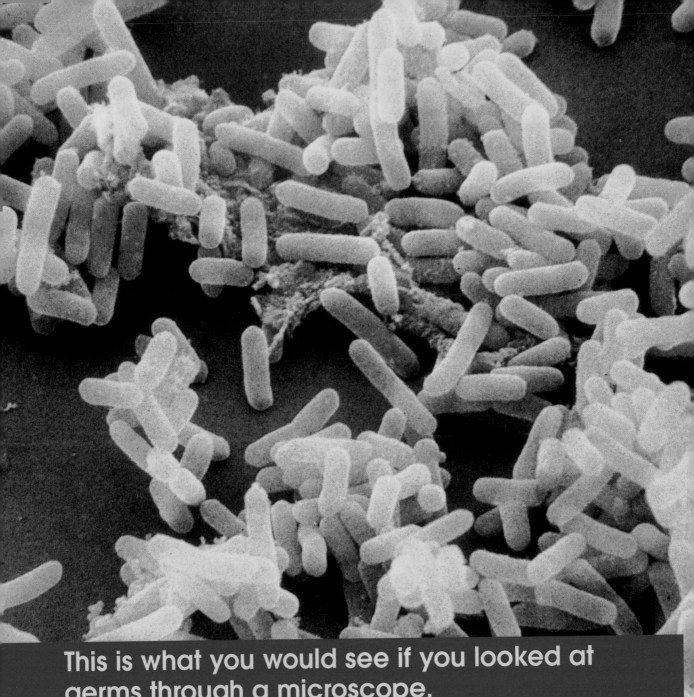

This is what you would see if you looked at germs through a microscope.

Germs Are Everywhere

Germs are small organisms that can make you sick. Germs live everywhere. Some germs even live inside your body. Keeping clean helps protect you from the germs that make you sick.

organism
a living plant or animal

Guess What?

Pets carry germs.
Remember to wash
your hands after you
play with a pet.

Washing Your Hands

Germs on your hands can get in your food or in your mouth. Washing your hands with soap and water cleans germs away. Wash your hands after you use the bathroom or blow your nose. Wash your hands before you eat.

Guess What?

The air that comes out of your nose when you sneeze can travel at speeds of 100 miles (160 kilometers) per hour.

Keeping Clean When You Are Sick

Keeping clean is important when you are sick. Throw away used tissues so you do not spread germs. Cover your mouth when you sneeze or cough. Wash your hands often when you are sick.

Why Do Feet Smell?

Your body sweats to keep cool. Some parts of your body sweat more than others. Your feet and armpits sweat a lot. Bacteria can grow in sweat. Bacteria sometimes smells bad.

bacteria
small organisms that can cause sickness and bad smells

Washing Your Body

Keeping your body clean helps you smell good. Take a shower or a bath several times each week. Washing your body with soap and water removes dirt and sweat.

Try This!

Comb your hair every day. Combing your hair removes tangles and helps keep your hair healthy.

Washing Your Hair

Keeping your hair and scalp clean is important. Washing your hair with shampoo helps rinse away dandruff and dirt. Wash your hair several times each week. Some people also use conditioner to make their hair soft.

dandruff
small, white flakes of dead skin from the scalp

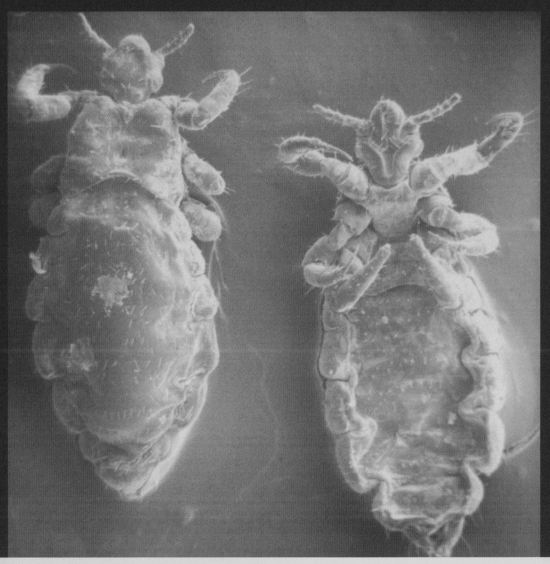

This is what you would see if you looked at head lice through a microscope.

Head Lice

Anyone can get head lice. Head lice are tiny parasites. They can live in human hair. Lice make your scalp itch. They also lay eggs called nits. Nits need to be combed out of hair. Lice must be killed with a special shampoo.

parasite
an animal or plant that gets its food by living on something else

Wearing Clean Clothes

Clothes get dirty and sweaty when you wear them. Washing your clothes is important. Wearing clean clothes, underwear, and socks helps you smell and look good. Keeping clean and wearing clean clothes help you feel good about yourself.

Hands On: Warm or Cold

Soap helps you keep clean. Water bounces off dirt and oil without soap. Soap helps the water break up the dirt and oil. This activity will show you whether soap works better in warm water or cold water.

What You Need

2 cups
Cold water
Warm water
Tablespoon
Vegetable oil
Liquid soap
Spoon

What You Do

1. Fill one cup with cold water.
2. Pour one tablespoon of vegetable oil into the water.
3. Add a few drops of liquid soap. Stir the water with the spoon.
4. Fill the other cup with warm water and repeat steps 2 and 3.
5. Does cold water or warm water help break up the oil more?

Soap works better in warm water. Use warm water when you clean yourself. It washes off the most dirt, oil, and germs from your body.

Words to Know

bacteria (bak-TIHR-ee-uh)—small organisms that can cause sickness and bad smells; bacteria can grow in sweat.

conditioner (kuhn-DISH-uh-nur)—a thick liquid used to make hair strong and soft

germ (JURM)—a small organism that can cause sickness; good hygiene protects you from germs.

organism (OR-guh-niz-uhm)—a living plant or animal; germs and bacteria are organisms.

scalp (SKALP)—the skin that covers the top of the head where hair grows

shampoo (sham-POO)—a soapy liquid used for washing hair

Read More

Lassieur, Allison. *Head Lice.* My Health. New York: Franklin Watts, 2000.

Royston, Angela. *Clean and Healthy.* Safe and Sound. Des Plaines, Ill.: Heinemann Library, 2000.

Internet Sites

BrainPop Movie: Hair
http://www.brainpop.com/health/integumentary/hair/index.weml

KidsHealth—What Are Germs?
http://www.kidshealth.org/kid/talk/qa/germs.html

Taking Care of Your Skin
http://kidshealth.org/kid/stay_healthy/body/skin_care.html

Index